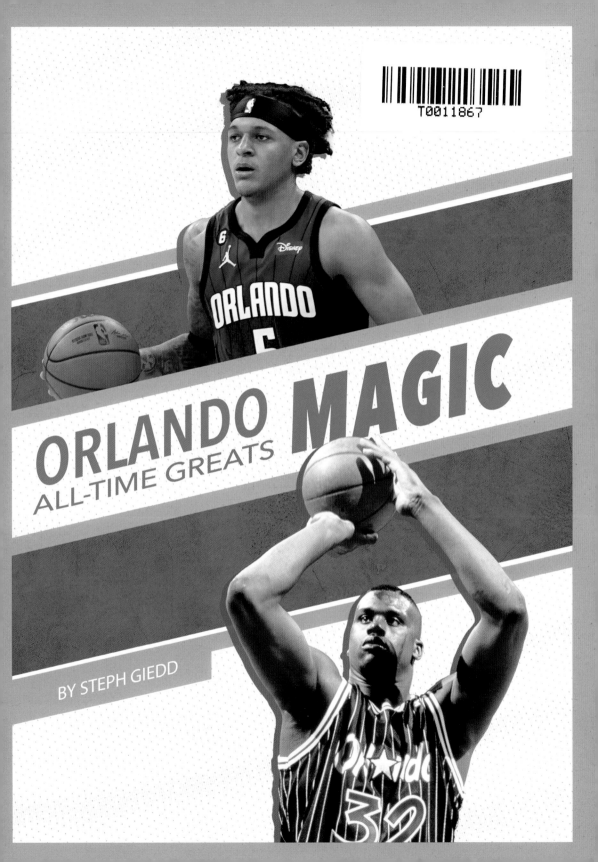

ORLANDO MAGIC
ALL-TIME GREATS

BY STEPH GIEDD

Book design by Jake Slavik
Cover design by Jake Slavik

Photographs ©: John Raoux/AP Images, cover (top), 1 (top), 20; Al Messerschmidt/AP Images, cover (bottom), 1 (bottom), 4, 6; Steve Simoneau/AP Images, 9; Don Frazier/AP Images, 10; Tony Ranze/AP Images, 13; Morry Gash/AP Images, 14; Kathy Willens/AP Images, 16; AJ Mast/AP Images, 19

Press Box Books, an imprint of Press Room Editions.

ISBN
978-1-63494-667-4 (library bound)
978-1-63494-691-9 (paperback)
978-1-63494-738-1 (epub)
978-1-63494-715-2 (hosted ebook)

Library of Congress Control Number: 2022919961

Distributed by North Star Editions, Inc.
2297 Waters Drive
Mendota Heights, MN 55120
www.northstareditions.com

Printed in the United States of America
082023

ABOUT THE AUTHOR

Steph Giedd is a former high school English teacher turned sports editor. Originally from southern Iowa, Steph now lives in Minneapolis, Minnesota, with her husband, daughter, and pets.

TABLE OF CONTENTS

CHAPTER 1
MAKING MAGIC

The Orlando Magic joined the NBA in 1989. They made shooting guard **Nick Anderson** their first draft pick. Anderson was an offensive spark in his 10 years with Orlando. He averaged 15.4 points per game over those years.

Point guard **Scott Skiles** was another original Magic player. He racked up 2,776

STAT SPOTLIGHT

ASSISTS IN A GAME
NBA RECORD

Scott Skiles: 30 (December 30, 1990)

O'NEAL
32

assists. That was the most in team history when he left in 1994. He also provided key leadership to the young team.

The Magic drafted **Dennis Scott** in 1990. He was never the Magic's biggest star. But the forward was a sharpshooter. He shot 40.3 percent from behind the arc with Orlando.

The Magic got their superstar when they selected center **Shaquille O'Neal** first overall in the 1992 draft. O'Neal was a force at 7'1" and more than 300 pounds. He averaged 27.2 points and 12.5 rebounds per game with the Magic.

O'Neal won Rookie of the Year in 1993. His arrival helped improve the team instantly. The Magic continued to surround their superstar with talent.

Guard **Anfernee "Penny" Hardaway** played a starring role. He was both a great passer and scorer. Hardaway had a major playoff run in 1995. He averaged 19.6 points and 7.7 assists per game.

Horace Grant was another key piece of this Magic era. The forward was tough in the paint. But he took care of the ball. Grant played seven seasons in Orlando. The Magic made the playoffs in all but one of them.

The highlight of this era came in 1994–95. With O'Neal leading the way, the Magic made the NBA Finals for the first time in their history. However, they were swept by the Houston

HARDAWAY
1

Rockets. O'Neal left after one more season in which Orlando won 60 regular season games. But the Magic couldn't make it back to the Finals. They tried to stay in contention by building around Hardaway. But it was soon clear a rebuild was needed.

ARMSTRONG
10

CHAPTER 2
HEART AND HUSTLE

By 2000, all of the Magic's key players had left Orlando. New coach Doc Rivers now had a roster that outworked its opponents. They became known as the "Heart and Hustle" Magic.

Point guard **Darrell Armstrong** was the perfect example of the "Heart and Hustle" attitude. He always offered effort off the bench. Upon becoming a starter in 1999–2000, he only got better. Armstrong won the Most Improved Player that season.

Joining the team after the "Heart and Hustle" season was guard **Tracy McGrady**. He was a tough player to defend. "T-Mac" could score from anywhere on the court. McGrady averaged an impressive 28.1 points per game with Orlando.

Point guard **Jameer Nelson** joined the Magic after McGrady was traded in 2004. Nelson played 10 years with the team as a steady passer and shooter. Turkish forward **Hedo Türkoğlu** also joined the Magic in 2004. At 6'10" he was a great scorer and passer for a big man.

The team was good but needed a superstar to be

DOC'S MAGIC

Doc Rivers coached the Magic for five seasons. In 1999–2000, Rivers made Orlando competitive without any superstars. He emphasized a hard-nosed style of play. Rivers was named NBA Coach of the Year with a 41–41 record.

MCGRADY
1

HOWARD
12

great. They got one through the 2004 draft in **Dwight Howard**. The center was already an All-Star two years later. He got the Magic back in the playoffs in 2007.

Forward **Rashard Lewis** joined the Magic in 2007–08. He gave them another shooting option. Lewis averaged 16.3 points per game with Orlando.

With all that talent, the Magic made it back to the Finals in 2009. But the Los Angeles Lakers offense was too powerful. The Lakers never gave the Magic a chance, despite strong play from Howard. They beat Orlando in five games.

STAT SPOTLIGHT

CAREER REBOUNDS
MAGIC TEAM RECORD
Dwight Howard: 8,072

VUČEVIĆ
9

CHAPTER 3
YOUNG AGAIN

The Magic traded Dwight Howard to the Los Angeles Lakers in 2012. One player who came to Orlando in the deal was big man **Nikola Vučević**. He became the team's leader for almost a decade. Vučević never hit the highs of Dwight Howard or Shaquille O'Neal. But he was a great scorer and an All-Star.

STAT SPOTLIGHT

REBOUNDS IN A GAME
MAGIC TEAM RECORD
Nikola Vučević: 29 (December 31, 2012)

Two promising forwards arrived in 2014 to play alongside Vučević. The Magic drafted **Aaron Gordon** fourth overall. He brought elite athleticism to the team.

Evan Fournier proved to be a strong shooter and a leader behind Vučević. They made the playoffs twice together. During Fournier's seven seasons with Orlando, he shot 38 percent from behind the arc.

However, the Magic still struggled. Late in the 2020-21 season, they traded Gordon, Fournier, and Vučević. Among the players Orlando got back was center **Wendell Carter Jr.** He quickly turned into a strong defender for the Magic. In 2021-22, he had his best NBA season to date. Carter averaged double digits in both points and rebounds per game for the first time in his career.

FOURNIER
10

ANTHONY
50

BANKING ON BANCHERO

Orlando drafted Paolo Banchero with the first overall pick in 2022. It was the fourth time the team had the top pick in the draft. The first three picks turned into All-Stars. The Magic selected Shaquille O'Neal in 1992, Chris Webber in 1993, and Dwight Howard in 2004. Webber never played for the Magic. He was traded for future team legend Penny Hardaway.

Carter joined a team with a young core. Orlando was already building around **Cole Anthony** as its point guard of the future. Anthony averaged 16.3 points per game in 2021–22 while taking over a starting role on a young Orlando team.

It was a talented roster. But the Magic still finished toward the bottom of the league. This earned them the first overall pick in 2022. Magic fans still had hope their young players would bring them back to the Finals.

TIMELINE

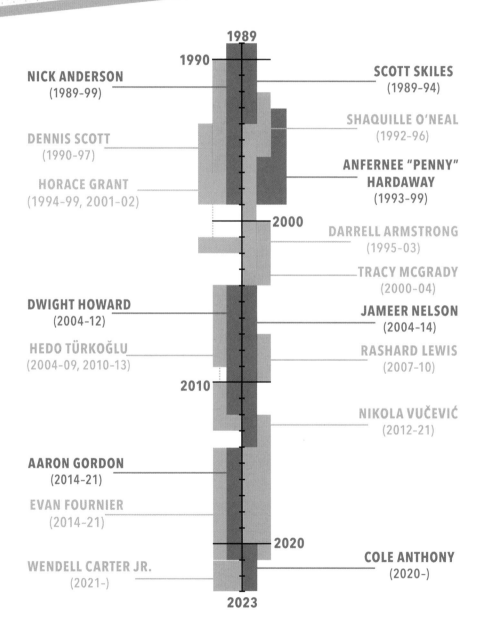

1989

1990

NICK ANDERSON
(1989-99)

SCOTT SKILES
(1989-94)

DENNIS SCOTT
(1990-97)

SHAQUILLE O'NEAL
(1992-96)

HORACE GRANT
(1994-99, 2001-02)

ANFERNEE "PENNY" HARDAWAY
(1993-99)

2000

DARRELL ARMSTRONG
(1995-03)

TRACY MCGRADY
(2000-04)

DWIGHT HOWARD
(2004-12)

JAMEER NELSON
(2004-14)

HEDO TÜRKOĞLU
(2004-09, 2010-13)

RASHARD LEWIS
(2007-10)

2010

NIKOLA VUČEVIĆ
(2012-21)

AARON GORDON
(2014-21)

EVAN FOURNIER
(2014-21)

2020

COLE ANTHONY
(2020-)

WENDELL CARTER JR.
(2021-)

2023

ORLANDO MAGIC

First season: 1989–90

NBA championships: 0*

Key coaches:

Brian Hill (1993–94 to 1996–97, 2005–06 to 2006–07) 267–192, 18–22 playoffs

Doc Rivers (1999–2000 to 2003–04) 171–168, 5–10 playoffs

Stan Van Gundy (2007–08 to 2011–12) 259–135, 31–28 playoffs

MORE INFORMATION

To learn more about the Orlando Magic, go to **pressboxbooks.com/AllAccess**.

These links are routinely monitored and updated to provide the most current information available.

Through 2021-22 season

GLOSSARY

assists
Passes that lead directly to a teammate scoring a basket.

athleticism
The combination of qualities such as speed, strength, and agility that an athlete has.

draft
An event that allows teams to choose new players coming into the league.

elite
The best of the best.

hard-nosed
Tough and determined.

paint
Another term for the lane, the area between the basket and the free throw line.

rookie
A first-year player.

sharpshooter
A player known for making many shots.

INDEX